MEDITATION

By Alan Watts

Book II in the Illustrated Series

THE ESSENCE OF ALAN WATTS

ALAN WATTS " . . . has provided a series
of sensitively illustrated jewel-books for
the searching spirits of this century . . . . "
—Joseph Campbell

Photographs by Joseph McHugh

CELESTIAL ARTS
Millbrae, California

Copyright©1974 by Celestial Arts
231 Adrian Road, Millbrae, California 94030

First Printing, July 1974
Second Printing, January 1975
Made in the United States of America

Cover photo of Alan Watts by Margo Moore
Photo on page 24 by Richard Borst
Photo on page 54 by Mark Watts
Photo on page 56 by Excelsior Incense

Library of Congress Cataloging in Publication Data

Watts, Alan Wilson, 1915-1973
    Meditation.

    (His The essence of Alan Watts, v.2)
    1.   Meditation. 2. Incense. I. Title
B945.W321 1974 vol.2 [BL627] 191s [291.4'3] 74-13647
ISBN 0-912310-76-6

THE STORY OF ALAN WATTS

For more than twenty years Alan Watts earned a reputation as the foremost interpreter of Eastern philosophies to the West. Beginning at the age of 20, when he wrote *The Spirit of Zen*, he developed an audience of millions who were enriched by his offerings through books, tape recordings, radio, television, and public lectures.

He wrote 25 books, each building toward a personal philosophy that he shared, in complete candor and joy, with his readers and listeners throughout the world. They presented a model of individuality and self-expression that can be matched by few contemporaries. His life and work reflect an astonishing adventure: he was editor, Anglican priest, graduate dean, broadcaster, and author-lecturer. He had fascinations for cooking, calligraphy, singing, and dancing. He held fellowships from Harvard University and the Bollingen Foundation and was Episcopal Chaplain at Northwestern University. He became professor and dean of the American Academy of Asian Studies in San Francisco, made the television series "Eastern Wisdom and Modern Life" for the National Educational Television, and served as visiting consultant to many psychiatric institutes and hospitals. He traveled widely with students in Japan.

Born in England in 1915, Alan Watts attended King's School Canterbury, served on the Council of the World Congress of Faiths (1936–38), and came to the United States in 1938. He held a Master's Degree in Theology from Seabury-Western Theological Seminary and an Honorary D.D. from the University of Vermont in recognition of his work in Comparative Religion.

Alan Watts died in 1973. *The Essence of Alan Watts*, a series of nine books in the unique *Celestial Arts* format, includes edited transcripts by his wife Mary Jane Watts of videotaped lectures that were produced by his friend, Henry Jacobs, and filmed by his son, Mark Watts, in the last years of his life.

The art of meditation is a way of getting into touch with reality. And the reason for meditation is that most civilized people are out of touch with reality. They confuse the world as it is with the world as they think about it, talk about it, and describe it. For on the one hand there is the real world and on the other a whole system of symbols about that world which we have in our minds. These are very, very useful symbols; all civilization depends on them. But like all good things, they have their disadvantages, and the principle disadvantage of symbols is that we confuse them with reality in the same way as we confuse money with actual wealth, and our names, ideas, and images of ourselves with ourselves.

Of course, reality from a philosopher's point of view is a dangerous word. A philosopher will ask what do I mean by *reality*—am I talking about the physical world of nature, or am I talking about a spiritual world, or what? I have a very simple answer: When we talk about the material world, that is actually a philosophical concept. In the same way, if I say that reality is spiritual, that's also a philosophical concept. And reality itself is not a concept. Reality is......(Sound of a gong). And we won't give it a name.

It's amazing what doesn't exist in the real world. For example, in the real world there aren't any things, nor are there any events. That doesn't mean the real world is a perfectly featureless blank! It means that it is a marvelous system of wiggles in which we descry things and events in the same way as we would project images on a Rorschach blot or pick out particular groups of stars in the sky and call them constellations. Well, there are groups of stars in our mind's eye in our system of concept, but they are not out there as constellations already grouped in the sky. In the same way, the difference between myself and all the rest of the universe is nothing more than an an idea—it is not a real difference. Meditation is a way in which we come to feel our basic inseparability from the whole universe. What that requires is that we shut up. We become interiorly silent and cease from the interminable chatter that goes on inside our skulls.

Most of us think compulsively all the time; we talk to ourselves. If I talk all the time I don't hear what anyone else has to say. In exactly the same way, if I think all the time, that is to say if I talk to myself all the time, I don't have anything to think about except thoughts. Therefore, I'm living entirely in the world of symbols and I'm never in relationship with reality. I want to get in touch with reality: That's the basic reason for meditation.

There is another reason, and this is a bit more difficult to understand. We could say that meditation doesn't have a reason or doesn't have a purpose. In this respect it's unlike almost all other things that we do except perhaps making music and dancing. When we make music we don't do it in order to reach a certain point, such as the end of the composition. If that were the purpose of music then obviously the fastest players would be the best. Also, when we are dancing we are not aiming to arrive at a particular place on the floor as in taking a journey. When we dance, the journey itself is the point, as when we play music the playing itself is the point. And exactly the same thing is true in meditation. Meditation is the discovery that the point of life is always arrived at in the immediate moment.

Therefore, if you meditate for an ulterior motive, that is to say to improve your mind, to improve your character, to be more efficient in life, you've got your eye on the future and you are not meditating. The future is a concept—it doesn't exist! There is no such thing as tomorrow! There never will be because time is always now. That's one of the things we discover when we stop talking to ourselves and stop thinking. We find there is only a present, only an eternal now.

One meditates for no reason at all except for the enjoyment of it. Here I would interpose the essential principle that meditation is supposed to be fun—it's not something you do as a grim duty. The trouble with religion today is that it is so mixed up with grim duties. You do it because it is *good for you*. It's a kind of self-punishment. Meditation when correctly done has nothing to do with all that. It's a kind of *digging* the present. It's a kind of *grooving* with the eternal now, it brings us into a state of peace where we can understand that the point of life, the place where it's at, is simply here and now.

The art of meditation uses various props or supports which should be mentioned. The first thing we are going to use as a means of stilling chatter in the mind is pure sound. And for that reason it is useful to have a gong. I have a Japanese Buddhist gong made of bronze and shaped like a bowl. You may buy one or make your own. Or you can use your own voice, chanting.

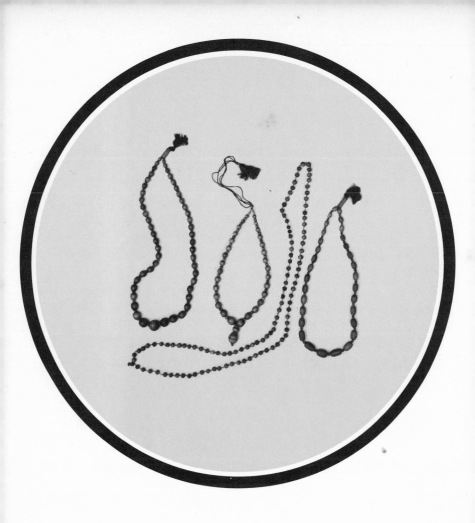

The second prop is a string of beads. These beads are used in meditation for an unconscious method of timing yourself. Instead of looking at a watch you move a bead each time you breathe in and out. And when you get to a certain rate of slow breathing, counting half the 108 beads on a rosary takes about 40 minutes. That is the usual length of time one sits in meditation, otherwise you become uncomfortable and get stiff legs and problems of that kind.

A third prop in meditation is the use of incense. The sense of smell is our repressed sense. Because it's our repressed sense, it has a very powerful influence on us and I will discuss it at length at the end of this book. Unconsciously we associate certain smells with certain states of mind, and since the smell of incense is associated with peace and contemplation, it's advantageous to burn incense in meditation.

Another thing that we should discuss is how does one sit in
meditation. You can sit any way you want—you can sit in a
chair, or you can sit like I sit which is the Japanese way,
kneeling with the toes pointing behind and sitting on the
heels in an upright posture, hands lying loosely in the lap. Or
you can sit in the lotus position, which is more difficult,
cross-legged with the feet on the thighs, soles upwards—and
the younger you begin practicing this the easier you find it to
do. You can just sit cross-legged on a raised cushion above
the floor if you prefer. The point is if you keep your back
erect—I don't mean stiff nor slumped—you are centered and
easily balanced and have the feeling of being rooted to the
ground. That sort of physical stability is very important for
the avoidance of distraction and generally feeling settled,
here and now. "Je suis, je reste," as the French say, "I'm here
and I'm going to stay."

Now that you are sitting and have your props, the easiest way to get into the meditative state is to begin listening. Simply close your eyes and allow yourself to hear all the sounds that are going on around you, listen to the general hum and buzz of the world as if you were listening to music. Don't try to identify the sounds you are hearing, don't put names on them, simply allow them to play with your ear-drums. Let them go. In other words, let your ears hear ˙ whatever they want to hear. Don't judge the sounds—there are no proper sounds nor improper sounds, and it doesn't matter if somebody coughs or sneezes or drops something—it's all just sound.

As you pursue that experiment you will very naturally find that you can't help naming sounds, identifying them, and go on thinking, talking to yourself inside your head, automatically. But it's important that you don't try to repress those thoughts by forcing them out of your mind because that will have precisely the same effect as if you were trying to smooth rough water with a flatiron—you're just going to disturb it all the more. What you do is this: As you hear sounds coming into your head, thoughts, you simply listen to them as part of the general noise going on just as you would be listening to cars going by, or to birds chattering outside the window. So look at your own thoughts as just noises. And soon you will find that the outside world and the inside world come together. They are a happening. Your thoughts are a happening just like the sounds going on outside, and everything is simply a happening and all you are doing is watching it.

In this process another happening that is very important is that you're breathing. As you start meditation you allow your breath to run just as it wills. In other words, don't do any breathing exercise, just watch your breath breathing the way it wants to breathe. And then notice a curious thing: You say in the ordinary way *I breathe* because you feel that breathing is something you are doing voluntarily just as you might be walking or talking. But you will also notice that when you are not thinking about breathing, your breathing goes on just the same. So the curious thing about breath is that it can be looked at both as a voluntary and an involuntary action. You can feel, on the one hand, *I am doing it* and, on the other hand, *it is happening to me.* And so, breathing is a most important part of meditation because it is going to show you, as you become aware of your breath, that the hard and fast division we make between what we do and what happens to us is arbitrary.

Watch your breathing and become aware that both the voluntary and the involuntary aspects of your experience are all one happening. That may at first seem a little scary. You may think *am I just the puppet of a happening, the mere passive witness of something that's going on completely beyond my control?* or *am I really doing everything that's going along?* If I were, I should be God and that would be very embarrassing because I would be in charge of everything—that would be a terribly responsible position! The truth of the matter is both things are true. Everything is happening to you, and you are doing everything. For example, your eyes are turning the sun into light, it's the nerve ends in your skin turning electric vibrations in the air to heat and temperature, it's your eardrums that are turning vibrations in the air into sound. This is the way in which you are creating the world. But when we're not talking about it, when we're not philosophizing about it, then there is just this happening, this...(Sound of a gong)...and we won't give it a name.

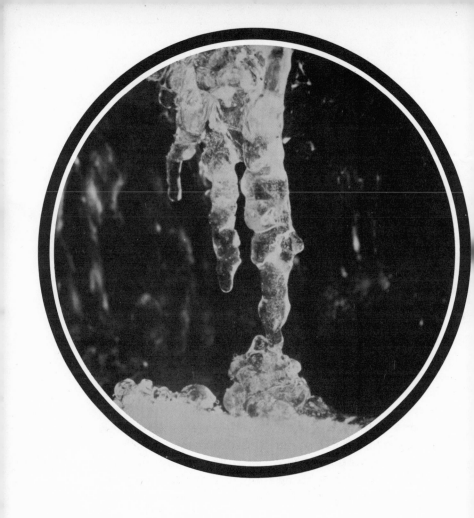

When you breathe for a while, just letting it happen and not forcing it in any way, you will discover a curious thing: Without making any effort you can breathe more and more deeply. Breathing out is important because it's the breath of relaxation as when we say, "Whew!" and heave a sigh of relief. So when you are breathing out you get the sensation that your breath is falling out. Dropping, dropping, dropping out with the same sort of feeling you would have if you were settling down into an extremely comfortable bed, you just get as heavy as possible and let yourself go. You let your breath go out in just that way. And when it's thoroughly, comfortably out and feels like coming back again, you don't pull it back in, you let it fall back in, letting your lungs expand, expand, expand until they feel very comfortably full. You wait a moment and let it stay there and then once again you let it fall out. In this way you will discover that your breath becomes naturally easier and easier and slower and slower, and more and more powerful.

Now you are listening to sound, listening to your own interior feelings and thoughts, and watching your breath all just as happenings that are neither voluntary nor involuntary. You are simply aware of these basic sensations. Then you begin to be in the state of meditation. Don't hurry anything, don't worry about the future, don't worry about what progress you're making. Be entirely content to be aware of what is. Don't be selective—"I should think of this and not that." Just watch whatever is happening.

To make this somewhat easier, to have the mind free from discursive, verbal thinking, chanted sound is extremely useful. If you, for example, simply listen to a gong, let that sound be the whole of your experience. It's quite simple, it requires no effort. And then along with that, or alone if you don't have a gong, you can use what in the Sanskrit language is called mantra. Mantras are chanted sounds which are used not for their meaning but for the simple tone, and they go along with slow breathing. One of the basic mantras is, of course, the word spelled OM. That sound is used because it runs from the back of your throat to your lips and contains the whole range of the voice and—it represents the total energy of the universe. This word is called the *pranava*, the name for the Ultimate Reality, for which than which there is no whicher. And so in this way then, if you chant it, *Ahhhhhhuuummmmmm*. And vary it *Ahhhhhhmmmm*, *Ahummmmmmm*, and keep it up for quite a long time and find that the words will become pure sound. You won't be thinking about it, you won't have any images about the sound going on in your mind. You will become completely absorbed in the sound and find yourself living in an eternal now in which there is no past and there is no future, and there is not difference between what you are as knower and what you are as the known, between yourself and the world of nature outside you. It all becomes one doing, one happening.

In addition to those slow moving chants you may find, according to your temperament, it is easier to do a fast moving one. These have a rhythm that is absorbing. A chant that you may have heard goes *Hari Krishna, Hari Krishna, Krishna Krishna, Hari Hari, Hari Krishna, Hari Krishna, Krishna Krishna, Hari Hari, Hari Rama Hari Rama, Rama Rama, Hari Hari, Hari Krishna, Hari Krishna, Krishna Krishna, Hari Hari...* And it doesn't matter what it means (Actually Krishna and Rama are the names of Hindu divinities.) The point is to get with that thing that is running, running, running... *Hari Krishna, Hari Krishna, Krishna Krishna, Hari Hari* and so on.

If you're a Christian or a Jew you may feel more inclined to use a meditation word that is more congenial to you, *Halleluja, Halleluja, Halleluja...*

41

If you are a Mohammedan you can use the Allah, the name of God. They have a way of doing it which gets very exciting: *Al-lah, Al-lah Al-lah Al-lah Al-lah Al-lah Al-lah Al-lah Al-lah Al-lah...* And it gets faster and faster and after 40 minutes you will be out of your mind.

But you see, to go out of your mind at least once a day is tremendously important. By going out of your mind you come to your senses. And if you stay in your mind all the time, you are overrational. In other words, you are like a very rigid bridge which because it has no give, no craziness in it, is going to be blown down in the first hurricane.

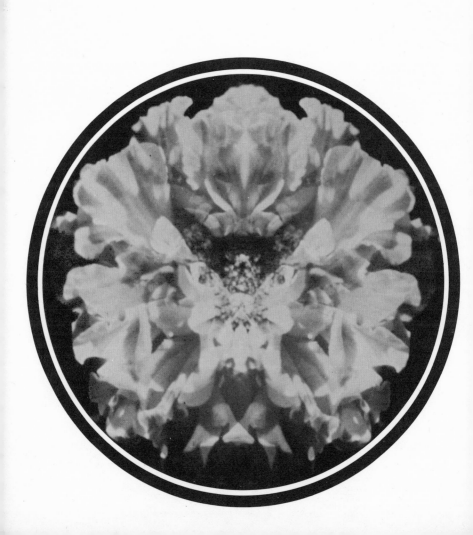

INCENSE

Trying to convey the idea of smells to you in words has the same sort of frustration one gets trying to describe color to the blind. I have a friend who was born blind. She has no idea what darkness is.

And so I had to try to give her an idea of what stars are and why we love them. I said, "Imagine when you touch the edge of something, you feel the edge, and then you move your hand away and nothing obstructs your hand, so there is space, nothing obstructing. Now imagine if you could put your hands out and feel around yourself a large collection of randomly distributed prickles, sharp points, that don't hurt you. At least not like the point of a needle. They're kind of pleasure-pain. We get this impression with the things we call our eyes, a friendly prickle coming at us from all over space when we can see them at night." So we try and translate the language of sight into the language of touch. Likewise we have this difficulty in talking about smell to people who, as G. K. Chesterton said, "They haven't got no noses, and goodness only knowses the noselessness of man."

Our sense of smell is not only repressed but is the one that we aren't really very proud of. For example, if I ask you "Do you smell?" It seems to be a rude question. There's a famous story about that great English literatus, Dr. Johnson, who got into a stagecoach one day (this was in the eighteenth century when people didn't bathe as much as they do today) and, shortly after, a lady got onto the stagecoach and sat opposite him, and said to him, "Sir, you smell." He said, "On the contrary, madam, you smell. I stink." And so you see how even in those times the word smell had a bad odor. There are only four adjectives in the English language that apply specifically to the sense of smell. We have acrid, pungent, fragrant, and putrid. We have ever so many adjectives from taste which we apply to smell, as when we say something smells sweet, or something of that kind. But we really aren't very conscious of the sense of smell. And yet it exercises an enormous influence upon us just because we're not conscious of it. I believe that instant likes and dislikes that we have for other people that are sometimes completely irrational are based on an unconscious determination of whether we do or don't like their smell. Smells are so powerful in evoking memories! Things you smelled as a child, say the smell of fresh coffee being cooked early in the morning, bacon frying, leaves being burned on an autumn day, all evoke vivid emotions and feelings of childhood.

But when people talk about very deep things, they never talk about the sense of smell. They talk about touch, vision, taste, and hearing. For example, we hear about the vision of God. In the Catholic Church it is said that the highest thing to which man can attain or to which the angels can attain is the beatific vision, to see God. One of the Psalms says, "Oh taste and see how excellent the Lord is." Taste and see. But no one ever had the idea of smelling God, of having not just the beatific vision, but the beatific aroma. Yet curiously enough, throughout the whole history of religions, until we got to what is called the phenomenon of the Protestant nose, we've used incense in our religious services.

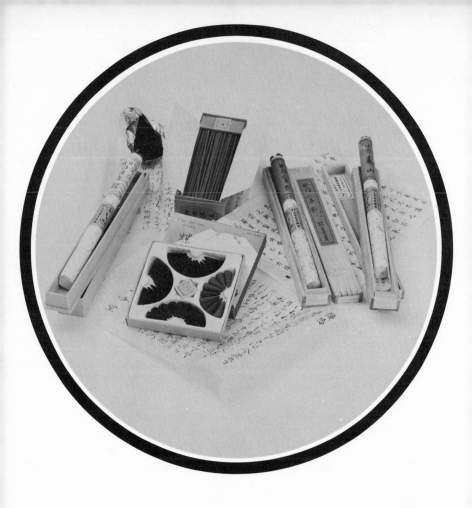

Hindus use incense, Buddhists use incense, Mohammedans use incense, Catholics use incense, Hebrews use incense or used to. But there came a break at the time of the Reformation when incense was somehow given up. And why is this? Why this repression of the sense of smell? I don't know, but I do know that it is repressed. That's a shame! We're depriving ourselves of a whole world of wonder. The nose is just as sensitive as the ears, and the same way as there can be glories for the eyes, there can be glories for the nose. I don't know why we're so diffident, so uptight about admitting that we have noses. Animals have the most incredible sense of smell and can detect all sorts of things. They open up to themselves a whole new world of experience by simply using their noses. Now if you don't use your nose, you're really in just as pitiable a condition as somebody who was born blind or deaf. You've lost a whole sense. So there is a whole art of smell. I know very little about one half of it: The art of perfumery. But I do know that a very skilled manufacturer of perfumes gets a very beautiful lady, sniffs the odor of her body and combines the natural odor of her body with a perfume ingredient that will be its perfect partner, producing some entirely individual scent that is her own authentic smell. I don't know why you shouldn't have your own authentic smell just as you have your own authentic voice, your own authentic face, and, indeed, your own authentic character. However, I do know quite a bit about incense.

Everybody knows that incense is widely sold in the United States and Europe. But the ordinary incense sold is usually black or purple in color. And although there are good incenses that are black and purple, I advise you never to buy a black or a purple incense, unless you're buying from someone who really understands incense and can advise you what to buy. But ordinarily, black or purple incenses smell like cheap perfume. A bad incense always has a soapy smell; a good incense has a woodsy, resinous, or floral smell. The absolutely basic incense for the Orient is sandalwood. I have a small trunk of sandalwood on which are written the Chinese characters, "Bird, Sound; Flower, Perfume." So, from the bird—sound, from the flower—perfume. Sometimes a piece of sandalwood is made into a statue, such as a Hindu goddess. But generally speaking, sandalwood is the basic incense. It comes in various forms—chips, powder, and sticks. The best way to burn incense is in a bowl with sand. Use charcoal, which you can buy from ecclesiastical shops, impregnated with saltpeter that lights itself. You can use ordinary barbecue charcoal but I don't recommend it. When you get the charcoal going, take a chip of incense wood and place it on the charcoal and slowly it will heat up. Soon you'll find the whole room marvelously impregnated with this curiously sweet, woodsy smell that isn't icky-sweet. There are three basic kinds of incense: temple incense, punk for scaring off insects, and boudoir incense. Temple incense is very pure; it has the feeling of high mountain forests, or loneliness—the chip form of sandalwood. There's the powder form of sandalwood which you just pinch on the lighted charcoal. You can use powdered sandalwood for rubbing into your hands. I wear round my neck what the Japanese call a juzu. It's a Zen Buddhist rosary. And you rub a little sandalwood powder into your hands and you play with it. I use them for counting my breath during meditation. You just breathe in and out on each bead, once out and once in. After you've counted each bead your whole rosary is perfumed with sandalwood.

Another wonderful kind of wooden incense comes from a
tree, which the Japanese call gingko, found in the Orient that
gets a disease which causes the wood to become extremely
hard. And that very hard wood, aloeswood is enormously
expensive. The disease in the tree is like the pearls in the
oyster—somehow out of disease comes something beautiful.
And you can burn aloeswood on charcoal. It has one of the
most marvelous perfumes in the world. Its smell is the high
forest, and old Dr. Suzuki, the great authority on Zen
Buddhism, said, "The smell of gingko is the smell of
Buddhism." It is used in Buddhist temples in China and Japan
for special occasions. There are so many other fantastic
varieties. There is a special incense which the Japanese use in
the peculiar custom of tea ceremony. It's a ceremony that is
nonreligious and yet very religious. Tea ceremony is drinking
tea, and there are no images, icons, or religious symbols
present. There is just drinking of tea in a completely, fully
attentive way, as if it were the only important thing in the
universe. Tea ceremony is completely living in the present,
being absolutely with what you're doing, but in a kind of
relaxed, easy way. Living in the eternal now, which is
actually the only place there is to be. For the ceremony the
Japanese use a particular vase with a curious little ivory top.
Originally it was a jar for pills or herbal medicine. The
masters of the tea ceremony felt that they were so elegant
that they came to be used as incense containers for the
ceremony. The incense is made of very small, black balls
with an absolutely distinctive smell that is associated with the
tea ceremony.

Another familiar form of incense is stick incense. Stick incense is lighted, the flame blown out, and stuck in a bowl of sand. The most luxurious of Japanese incense is based on musk although it's green, which is usually pine. Also, you can find, although it's rare, amazing stick incense from Tibet. It's regarded as a punk. Punk has the smell of autumn leaves. It is a little richer and is very good for keeping away mosquitoes. There is a similar, marvelous incense stick from Nepal. It is a coarse incense that I have a special liking for, it is distinct from the ones that are too icky-perfumed. One of the most extraordinary ones from Nepal comes in the form of a little piece of rope. This has a good-sweet flavor as distinct from icky-sweet. It's like the sweetness of fresh strawberries or fine honey compared to the sweetness of cheap candy.

Pakistan has a spiral incense which is a punk, used for keeping away mosquitoes. There's another interesting form of spiral incense which is used to reproduce a religious symbol, or whatever, when lighted it burns until the symbol is outlined in black.

In the West, the principle incense in use is resin. Frankincense, a resin, is really basic to incenses used in the Christian churches both of the East and of the West. And the delightful thing about using frankincense is the censer or thurible which you swing to disperse the incense. It's charming to use, and you can swing it right around without the incense coming out. It is used this way throughout the Western churches and, for reasons unknown to me, the Protestants gave it up. They lost all the joy of doing this thing for the greater glory of God.